THOUGHT CATALOG BOOKS

Big Heart Problems

Big Heart Problems

MARISA DONNELLY

THOUGHT CATALOG BOOKS

Brooklyn, NY

THOUGHT CATALOG BOOKS

Copyright © 2016 by The Thought & Expression Co.

All rights reserved. Published by Thought Catalog Books, a division of The Thought & Expression Co., Williamsburg, Brooklyn. Founded in 2010, Thought Catalog is a website and imprint dedicated to your ideas and stories. We publish fiction and non-fiction from emerging and established writers across all genres. For general information and submissions: manuscripts@thoughtcatalog.com.

First edition, 2016

ISBN 978-1530386598

10 9 8 7 6 5 4 3 2 1

Cover photography by © KJ Parish

Contents

1.	19 Things Only Girls Who Can't Help Falling In Love Over And Over Again Can Relate To	1
2.	I Want A Love As Euphoric As A Runner's High	5
3.	To The Boyfriend I Planned My Life With, This Is For You	9
4.	If You Are The Wind	13
5.	16 Rules For Falling In Love With A Writer	15
6.	I Want Your Monday Mornings	19
7.	Trying To Move On	21
8.	This Is How It Feels When You Love Someone Who Struggles With Depression	23
9.	I Want You On A Sunday Afternoon	27
10.	This Is How You Will Miss Me	29
11.	Don't Settle For The Nice Guy	31
12.	Read This If You Love Someone Who Doesn't Trust You	35
13.	Breaking Up Meant Saying Goodbye To The Home That Was Never Really Mine	39
14.	It's Not You, It's Me… I Think	43
15.	To The Next Girl He Loves	45
16.	This Is The Incredible Power Of Love After Loss	47
17.	You Broke My Heart, But I Am Forever Thankful	51
18.	This Is What Is Left When You Lose Someone You Love	55
19.	I Made A Million And One Mistakes Loving Him, And I Will Make Them All Again	57
20.	10 Reasons Why The Best Relationship Of Your Life Will Be With A Girl Who Loves 'Too Much'	61
21.	Love Is Easy, It's Loving That's Hard	65
22.	I'm A Spoiled Brat Because I Want You To Love Me As Much As I Love You	71

23. It's Okay To Love Fiercely (And Expect Fierce Love In Return)   73

1

19 Things Only Girls Who Can't Help Falling In Love Over And Over Again Can Relate To

1. The cousin that always asks, "So, who are you in love with *this* year?"

2. The collection of scrapbooks tucked beneath your bed or at the bottom of the closet representing so many brief but passionate relationships past. And the robust sticker collection ("hugs and kiss," "be mine," etc.) just in case you need to make another.

3. It takes at least three months to mourn a break-up. With some minor exceptions. Like if you find true love before the three-month mark, of course.

4. Soul connections are a real thing. You'll deny it, but you ultimately really do believe this.

5. You have a Pinterest board dedicated to your existing Boyfriend/Future Hubby. And a Miss Independent board for the periods in between dating future husbands.

6. "Wow, you're in *another* serious relationship?"

7. You have three canned answers ready at all times in case anyone asks you about your relationship status: a.) It's complicated, b.) I'm not sure where things will go, and c.) He's *definitely* The One.

8. You regularly have to deny that you ever claimed your last boyfriend was "*definitely* The One."

9. Alone time sounds like a good idea, except compared to cuddling.

10. Your excuse for jumping into a new relationship: "Honestly, I'm not sure how it all happened. But he's a *really* good guy. This one's different."

11. You aren't so sure about the whole marriage thing. But you have big plans for it. And a Pinterest board dedicated to your hypothetical wedding.

12. Inner thoughts while staring at your latest boyfriend: *Can I see myself married to this guy? Because if not than this is pointless, right?*

13. You love solitude—going for a run, pigging out on tacos, watching TV by yourself—but you really only pursue those solo activities when you're single, or your significant other is out of town.

14. You have two sets of travel plans: One trip in case you're dating someone, and another in case you end up having to fly solo.

15. You also have two separate sets of plans for the future: the 'If We Break Up' list, and the 'My Life With Him' list.

16. "Yeah, things are moving pretty fast," and "When you know you just *know*," seem to creep their way into a lot of conversations you have.

17. Your best friend from childhood always leads with: "Okay, so give me the scoop. Who's the new guy?"

18. There are three love-related playlists on your phone at all times: 'Lovey Dovey,' 'Sad Breakup Songs,' and 'Single and Lovin' It.'

19. Every time you see a post about being young and in love, you nod your head in agreement and click through so you can imagine yourself hugging your latest boyfriend at sunset like the happy couple in the accompanying photograph (even though you've done this with at least a dozen guys in mind before).

2
I Want A Love As Euphoric As A Runner's High

I took a deep breath and quickened my pace, staring straight ahead at a small sliver of sunset, barely visible between a line of evergreen trees. I focused on that sky, on the purply-pinks fading to navy, and regulated my breathing. In through my nose, deep, until it filled every empty space and capillary of my lungs. Then out slow through my mouth. And I started sprinting.

I could feel my legs, my arms, my chest expanding like a weightless balloon, but I stared straight ahead. I didn't break focus. The outline of the trees stayed sharp; the pine needles let glimmers of evening light through, their thick bodies swaying ever so slightly in the breeze.

I took a deep breath and could feel the goosebumps wash over me. This was it—the moment all runners crave, better than any high—the adrenaline and euphoria that comes in a chill from your head all the way to your pounding feet. It washed over me suddenly, taking away any feeling of exhaustion or soreness or tightness.

I could only feel my breath filling my lungs and a fuzzy, lightness of my legs. I was weightless.

This is what I crave in every single run: *the high*. The moment my mind and my body drift outside themselves and connect in some far-off, euphoric runner's wonderland. I lose all outside thought noise or music or pain and I just *run*. Repetition of legs and arms and feet and breath.

I lose myself in the sudden energy, strength, and grace I feel. Everything else is obsolete.

I want a love like this runner's high.

I want a love that washes over me when I least expect it. A love that grabs hold of every part of me—my brain, my heart, my body—and makes me shiver. A love that demands my attention, yet leaves me in control. A love that's euphoric, incredible, and breath-taking, yet steady. I am caught in the whirlwind, but safe, always able to take deep breaths.

I want a love that fills me from the inside out. That starts with a small moment of focus and expands outward, through pain and fear and outside worry. A love that zeroes in and washes away everything else, leaving me and that person and that moment. Bliss.

I want a love that challenges me, that pushes me. That takes me beyond the basic jog to a sprint. That's going to make my body burn, but also blossom. That will make me determined and strong and faithful to that beautiful feeling. Keep coming back because I cannot live without that powerful, weightless feeling.

Running, loving—we're all chasing some kind of high. But I want a love that gives me the same feelings a sprint does—terrifying and perfect.

3

To The Boyfriend I Planned My Life With, This Is For You

When I close my eyes, I can still picture your apartment—the kitchen with the dirty stove, the bathroom littered with crumpled tissues and bath soap, the bedroom with abandoned sweatshirts and sweatpants like land mines around the bed. I remember the tie blanket with the football print, the coin jar on the nightstand, your hand with the silver bracelet around my waist.

You were him. The one. Or at least I thought. We spent our nights curled up on the couch—me and my homework, you and Sports Center. Our Saturday afternoons were spent cooking breakfast burritos and arguing. Your stubbornness matched mine in ways that always made me question how we even ended up together. But we did, somehow.

You were the one I traveled with, West Coast to Midwest, swimsuits to wool mittens. We talked about our dreams on plane rides, mapped our futures together on lazy Sunday mornings before church.

You were the one I planned my life with. Graduate. Move.

Travel. I fit your life into mine like silly putty, oozing it into the cracks and empty spaces. I was young. I was busy. You were older, your life not put together, but at a different stage than mine. I was ready to sift through my life and make room for you. You were ready to take our lives and mesh them together. But then you were the one who pulled away.

Our lives weren't compatible. Our arguments turned to fights. Our futures drifted apart, the glue holding them together becoming weak and stringy. I made my life more complicated, my schedule filling with work and goals, and yours, 4,000 miles away, could have been another world.

We broke up on a Saturday, the weekend after Father's Day. I remember the feeling. I was dressed in a thin tank-top and scarf, the June heat making my hair frizzy. I tried so hard not cry. I was watching the horse races, squeezed between my mother and sister in little bleacher seats. I watched the horses circle the track, their chiseled leg muscles gleaming in the sunlight. They were resilient.

I felt my life crumbling around me, pieces of who I thought I was getting lost in the voices of the racetrack, mixing with the smell of beer, and popcorn, and lady's perfume.

You were the one I planned my life with, imagined myself at twenty-six, thirty-five, forty-two with children. I shaped my dreams around yours. No longer mine, but ours. And I loved you.

But maybe not enough. Or maybe too much. Our lives were

not matched, not in the way they should have been. I still think about you sometimes, wonder if you still have that coin jar on your dresser, if you still have that silver bracelet, and wonder if, in the back of your nightstand drawer, you have a picture of the two of us. And maybe you still wonder sometimes what could have been.

4
If You Are The Wind

If you are the wind
then I am stretching
myself across you,
with you
weightless
arms open, like sails.
If you are the wind
then I am whispers, lost,
coalescing, transforming into one
quiet rush. Silence.
If you are the wind
then I am the soaring bird
wings beating, heart
pumping, matching stroke
for gust.
If you are the wind
than I am the dandelion seed, twisting
spinning, caught
in your embrace
traveling miles, seeing a sky
of which I'd never dreamed.

But you are not the wind.
And I am standing on the edge

of a hill, watching the snowflakes
swirl around me,
my face pink
and cold.

5
16 Rules For Falling In Love With A Writer

Rule #1: Take things slow. We are complex (which is code for difficult sometimes). We have layers, and we hide behind each of them. Behind our characters, behind our lines of poetry, behind the narration in our heads. (No, we're not crazy. Not too crazy, anyway.) But to love us, you have to scratch at the surface, pull each layer back, then we'll fall. Suddenly. All at once. (Be prepared).

Rule #2: Try to understand us. We don't always make sense, but our writing will. (So you should probably read it.)

Rule #3: Give us plenty of space. We like to breathe, to think, (AKA: overthink) and reflect. It doesn't mean we don't love you. We just value our alone time just as much as our you-and-me time.

Rule #4: Listen to us when we're inspired. And even if we talk your ear off, for the sake of our (and your) sanity, let us.

Rule #5: Tell us sweet nothings. And sweet everythings. And words in-between. Tell us about your days, your job, your life. Tell us stories about the person you used to be. Tell us dreams about who you want to become. This motivates us, makes us love you even more, and will probably weave its way into one of our characters.

Rule #6: Allow yourself to be vulnerable. Let us pick at the best pieces of you and love each of them.

Rule #7: Challenge us. Don't be a stock character in one of our stories, but make us think. Let us learn from you, grow with you, and become better alongside you.

Rule #8: Read what we write. (Refer to Rule #2) Ask us what we're writing about. But most important: read. And if you don't understand, then ask. We love to talk about what we do. And we love making you a part of it.

Rule #9: Inspire us. With your thoughts and opinions, with the last thing you heard or read, or just with your random ideas. (You're more creative then you think, by the way.)

Rule #10: Accept (and appreciate) that we are passionate and emotional. And never give us crap for this. Ever.

Rule #11: Engage in conversations. With us, with our crazy writer-friends, with our mutual friends, and with our families. Be an active part of our lives and what we talk about. It will bring us closer. (And then you'll see more love poems. Guaranteed.)

Rule #12: Forgive us. For the snippets of you that find their way into a plot line, for the secrets you've whispered that somehow made it to the page. We're passionate about both things—our words and you—sometimes we can't keep them apart.

Rule #13: Love us. When we're down, when we can't find the right words, when we're stressed with deadlines, when we're uninspired. Give us kisses and hugs, back rubs, a book of poems, or even just your hand. Love opens our heart. And our heart unlocks our words.

Rule #14: Believe in us. Even when we aren't making the big bucks (because we most likely won't) and more importantly, when we don't believe in ourselves. You're our lifeline. Even if we don't actually tell you that.

Rule #15: Fight with us. Tell us when we're wrong. Argue when you're right. You'll teach us about love and its challenges. You'll make us stronger, brain and heart. (And you'll give us more things to write about.)

Rule #16: And give yourself some credit. We're a tough breed. But we have big hearts. And we love you. Just know that even if our brains are filled with words most of the time, a good chunk of those words are about you. And every day we're writing our love story—real, and on the page.

6

I Want Your Monday Mornings

The mornings when your head is spinning with alarms, deadlines, and to-do lists. When you pace furiously around the kitchen, when you leave the dirty dishes in the sink, when you feel like you're continuously running out of time. That's when I want you the most.

I want to grab your arm and pull you to me, feel the muscles in your back, run my fingers through your hair and kiss the soft skin between your collarbone and neck.

I want to breathe calm air into your lungs, to slow your heart down, to keep you rooted with me, here in this moment.

I want to kiss you until your eyes close. To pull you back to bed with me and tuck the covers around you until you're calm and warm.

I want to tell you I love you, and hear you respond, thick and slow, your voice coated with sleep.

I want your Monday mornings. When your mind is elsewhere, when you're distracted and busy and anxious and stressed. I want your thoughts, your insecurities, your fears. I want you in all your vulnerability and craziness, your dread and irritation. I want the real you. When push comes to shove and you're sick and tired of being sick and tired, I want all of you. Just like that.

And I want to be the kiss, the touch that centers you. Regulates your heart beat. Keeps you in control. Keeps you going.

7
Trying To Move On

He had blue eyes and blonde hair,
laughter that filled the room and a smile
that was dizzying.
Late at night she dreamed of this,
of someone new slipping
into her life like a sun-kissed angel.
They hadn't met before, just two
twenty-somethings smiling
over a shot of whiskey.
Paths crossed, air hot
with drunken electricity.
She hadn't pictured this exact moment,
but had hoped it would be
something like this.
His thick coat over her shoulders,
Jack warm in their bellies.
Outside, the night sky was white
with snow flurries.
Each flake fell and kissed
her cheeks, then melted,
fleeting.

8

This Is How It Feels When You Love Someone Who Struggles With Depression

Like you're standing in the middle of a concert, bodies jumping and screaming all around you, and you're desperately trying to push through to grab your person's hand. But you can't. The concert is wild, and you're getting tossed and pushed around. And no matter how much you squeeze and shimmy and elbow, their fingertips are just out of reach. Every time.

Like you're running in place. A step up, a step down. Unmoving. Stuck.

Like you're underwater, trying to speak, but your words come out mumbled and off-key and you keep opening your mouth and it fills with water so you can't speak. And the person you love is just floating, slowing sinking down, down.

When you love someone with depression your heart becomes achy and heavy. You cannot begin to fathom their pain, but you try so very hard. You try to hold them, try to package them into a little box and keep them safe. But you just can't.

You understand that their pain is something you cannot change, but you try anyways. You tell them positive things, you try to lift their burdens, you do your best to keep them distracted and laughing to the point that you're physically exhausted and empty. But you love them, so you keep trying.

When you love someone with depression, you get frustrated and bitter. And then you hate yourself for it. You want to pull that person out of their own head, but it's a decision you can't make for them. So you hang onto their words, hoping, praying that things will turn around. You stand on the sidelines as they get help, as they take little steps forward, then giant leaps back. You want to grab them and carry them across the finish line, the 'happy' line. You want to lift them and travel back in time to where they used to be. But you are powerless. So you wring your hands and cheer from the sidelines and pray.

When you love someone with depression, it's like you're driving an open, empty road with no clear destination. You try to get off the path, to change direction, but you're just not sure where to head, or if the road will be clear once you make that left turn.

You try to be tender, but not baby them. Try to be normal, but not too normal that you forget what they're struggling with. You aren't sure what to feel, or how to talk, or what to do. And sometimes you feel like giving up yourself. Those are the hardest days.

But you don't give up. You continue speak, even if your words fall on closed ears. You continue to comfort, even if your care seems useless. You continue to love, because that's all you can do. Love and pray and be there, physically and mentally and in all other ways. Be there. So even if that person doesn't know happiness, they know they're not alone.

9
I Want You On A Sunday Afternoon

I want the lazy way you roll out of bed, or back into bed, your arm draping over the blanket and your body semi-curled up, though you'll furiously deny that's how you sleep.

I want the fresh-out-of-the-shower you, hair dripping and wet feet making a puddle on the linoleum.

I want the brunch-in-bed you, the *come cuddle me* you, the sleepy, dreamy kisses on my cheek you.

When your half-asleep and pull me closer to your chest, I want that.

When you come home from church and your head's filled with wonderful, crazy ideas and verses, I want that.

When you're nestled on the couch with two different socks and a leftover slice of pepperoni pizza watching football, I want that.

I want the you with your hair unbrushed, shirt untucked, and eyes heavy with sleep. I want the you that doesn't demand attention, that is content holding me, that thinks the world of us and wants nothing than to spend time together, talking, cuddling, being lazy.

Yes, I want you on a Sunday afternoon.

When the windows are cracked and the breeze blows in, when the blankets are pooled around us, when we have nowhere to be and hours to learn each other's minds and hearts—that's when I want you.

Yes, I want you in all the ways—a Friday at the bar, a Saturday out with friends, a Tuesday night when we're both exhausted from work. But I especially want you on a Sunday. On a day without obligations, plans, schedules. An afternoon that seems like it's created just for us, for warm skin, fingertips intertwined, my legs on your lap and two glasses of wine on the table. The hours stretched out like promises, an eternity to fall in love.

10

This Is How You Will Miss Me

You will miss me in the mornings
when your bed is cold and empty.
You will miss me as the leaves change
and the swings rest still,
untouched.
You will miss me in the chipped
coffee mug, in the worn path
where my car used to park, in the blank faces,
empty beer cans, long nights waking to the sound
of someone else's heavy breathing.
You will miss me in all forms. Quiet
and loud. When you're in a crowd
of people, drunkenly singing
to a country song or alone in the shower
humming to a tune on shuffle
and the water hits
your skin, sends shivers
down the muscles in your back.
You will miss me when you least expect it.
In the softness of a blanket, at a stoplight,
in the lines of my handwriting
on a piece of paper you find at the bottom

of your drawer. And then you will remember
the sound of my voice, the warmth of my lips
on your skin, my hair mixed with yours,
my brown, brown eyes.
This is how you will miss me
and how you will remember me in all the ways
I will never remember myself.
Because I am no longer her
anymore.

11

Don't Settle For The Nice Guy

Don't settle for the nice guy. For the guy who buys you a shiny necklace at Christmas time and wraps it in a box with a big red bow. For the guy who gives you the last sour cream and onion chips from his lunch. For the guy who sends you page-long good morning texts.

Don't settle for the guy who tells you you're pretty. For the guy who buys you roses when you argue. For the guy who always takes you to a steak dinner on your anniversary.

Fall for the guy that keeps you on your toes. The one whose gifts you can never anticipate—a road trip to the mountains, concert tickets, a picnic lunch. The one that gives you the gift of his time, taking you places, showing you pieces of his childhood like a map you can one day trace.

Fall for the guy who doesn't just leave you his last chips, but shares the whole bag. And the glass of root beer, sip for sip from the same straw.

Fall for the guy who doesn't just send you good morning texts, but tells you in person. Who absentmindedly twists your curls around his finger when you're watching a movie.

Who attempts to braid your hair even though he has no idea how. Who pushes your bangs back from your face to kiss you. Who stops and just smiles at you—when you're walking to the grocery store, stepping through the door after a run, on your hands and knees scrubbing the bathtub—and tells you he loves you.

Fall for the guy who doesn't call you 'pretty,' but calls you beautiful, smart, intelligent, strong. Who treats you like a person, not an object to be admired. Who keeps a picture of you in his wallet and tells his mother, his best friend how wonderful you are, not just how good you look.

Fall for the guy that you fight with. Dramatically. Passionately. But not the guy who will buy you roses in attempt to patch things without truly fixing them. Fall for the guy who will compromise. Who will stay up late talking things over. Who will forgive. Who will apologize. Who will say the words, 'I'm sorry' and not hide behind a 50 character message attached to a rose stem.

Fall for the guy that cooks. Or tries to cook. For the guy who looks up new restaurants to take you, from Mongolian to Greek, in the middle of the city to the outskirts of town. Fall for the guy who brings you Chinese takeout when you're feeling lazy, or makes homemade chicken soup when your throat hurts.

Don't settle for the nice guy. For the guy who says all the right things. The one who sweeps you off your feet but doesn't scare you. Fall for the guy who challenges you, who argues with you, who pushes you to think differently, to be a better person, to do something you haven't done. Fall for the guy who is passionate, emotional, imperfect. Fall hard and never settle. Ever.

12

Read This If You Love Someone Who Doesn't Trust You

Trust is a fragile thing. You've probably heard that before. You've also probably heard *trust is earned, not given.* Or *trust is everything.* Or maybe even *trust is like an eraser; it gets smaller with every mistake.* Regardless, the idea of trust is the most basic, yet essential part of every single relationship. It is the spine, the backbone of what it means to love another person.

When you trust someone, you allow yourself to be vulnerable. You let that person in. You give that person your heart, your entire soul, and believe, despite all of the crap in the world, that they will take care of it.

You watch that person walk away and you have confidence that they are respectable and won't go throwing themselves around or flirting behind your back or opening themselves to any other human besides you. But the thing about trust, is that it relies so much on the unknown. It is a testament of faith, that despite the odds and no matter what the world says, you believe the person you love will do you no harm.

Damn. That takes strength.

In today's world, trust is difficult. It's either given too freely, or withheld too much. Oftentimes a person gets hurt, thus they puts up that don't-mess-with-me wall. This is understandable, right? (To some extent.) When we are broken, we are bitter. We don't want to let someone else in, even if that person looks like an angel because we know about fallen angels. We know about heartbreak. We know how it feels to be crushed, shattered, damaged, betrayed. So we don't trust. We keep ourselves closed like little roly-poly bugs, folding inside ourselves as soon as we might be close enough to really feel something.

After time, we open. Layer by layer, to love. We learn how it feels to love someone again, but we still don't trust. Not yet. Which is the real problem. You can't truly love without trust. Any relationship that isn't built with a secure foundation of faith will break.

So here you are. You are in love with someone that doesn't trust you. This person pulls you in close, and wants to keep you there, suffocated under the guise of 'protected'. They want to know everything about where you're going, who you're with, what you're wearing, why you're friends with so-and-so and if you're lying. Because you're probably lying, right? (Wrong.) They make you question yourself. They make you doubt yourself. They make you look at the mirror and wonder if you're as shady of a person as they make you out to be. (You're not, just so you know.)

The way they treat you is the complicated mess of their life.

Their before-you life, their broken life. Whoever they used to love betrayed them and they are no longer the same. So they question you. They doubt you. They probably do behind your back exactly what they accuse you of doing because they're afraid of getting hurt again. And that sucks.

But it's not your problem. Yes, you love this person. Yes, you are loyal to this person. Yes, you are honest and would never hurt them and care so deeply for them and their broken, painful past. But you are someone who is worthy of trust. And the baggage that this person carries, drags like dead weight is only that—dead weight.

Your SO's trust issues are not your problem. Sure, you can comfort this person and teach them what real love is, but you cannot change their mindset. You cannot spend your life trying to prove that you are different, that you love them, that you are not like the last girl or guy who changed their belief in love. You cannot bend over backwards for them, change your clothing for them, drop your friends for them, stay at home for them, ignore plans for them, shift your world view for them, or become new for them. Because that would not be fair to you. And really, the issues they're having have nothing to do with you at all.

So what do you do? You are patient, at first. You show them the person you are and you teach them what trust looks like, how freeing and wonderful and powerful it is to let go of insecurities and rely on someone to carry your heart in the palm of their hands. Hopefully they see the beauty in that. See that you are not their ex, not the person that changed them, not the person that shattered their entire world, but a new beginning.

But if they still question you, if they still watch your every move, if they still say terrible things to you and about you because they don't have faith in the person you are, you need to free yourself. You need to let go of the idea that you can change their thinking. They must change it themselves. So you set yourself free. And in doing so, you free them, too. So that they can grow, rebuild, and become whole enough to love and trust the next beautiful soul that enters their life.

13

Breaking Up Meant Saying Goodbye To The Home That Was Never Really Mine

To the house that was never my house:

I learned a lot from your paint-chipped walls, from your groaning heater, from your kitchen with the spray painted window and the pile of dishes always in the sink.

You were the home of the boy I loved. The boy whose hands intertwined with mine on the edge of your roof, whose hips kissed mine, side by side on the sunny patch of grass next to your back door.

It was you that taught me to love again. You, that gave me comfort within your walls. You that gave me both a place and a person to call home.

As the months passed, your creaking steps became familiar, the carpet a soft padding underneath my tired feet.

Your worn leather couch was my resting place. I watched TV, I watched college students take shots, I watched my world grow and crumble and change simultaneously. As I fell in love, as I lost myself, as I felt alone at a party in a sea of faces I could no longer recognize.

Your front steps were where I first held the boy I loved, kissed his cheek. Your upstairs bedroom was where I first said, 'I love you.' And your bathroom was where I cried after him and I fought.

You know my secrets, House That Was Never Mine. The thoughts that creep into my mind at night when I'm alone in that upstairs bedroom, wishing for something different. Wishing to be loved more fully.

You see my face in that dirty mirror, reflecting back again and again and again. A hundred different faces with a blank expression. Searching.

You taught me to see life differently. That the exterior of anything does not determine its value. That a place is only a home because of a feeling. That when you love a person their space becomes yours. You become that space. Interchangeable. Intertwined. So much so that you are no longer you, when you aren't a part of it.

I miss you, House That Was Never Mine. I miss the way your lights were always on, the television always a background noise, the piano always out of tune. I miss my shoes by the front door, a reminder that I belonged.

I miss the boy that I loved, whose face was always hidden in the shadow of that upstairs bedroom light. You taught me to believe in him. To trust creaking staircases and dirty floors. To believe in the words, 'I'm in love with you,' as the sunlight peeked through your curtained window.

You may not be mine anymore. But House That Was Never Mine, you will always feel like home.

14

It's Not You, It's Me... I Think

It's not you, it's me. I think, as I watch the wind blow slits of sunlight through the big pine tree in my backyard. You love me in all the right ways: the hand-holding, the forehead kisses, the tenderness, the love that fills me. But you suck at all the other boy things, like taking me on dates or cleaning your room.

But it's not you, it's me. It's the way I can't stop wishing for things I don't have, the way my life feels like an open road or a blank canvas and I'm the only one with shoes, with a pen. It's not the way you make me laugh, it's the way I want to spend every minute discovering what makes me laugh. It's not the way you make me smile, it's how I want to learn what else makes me smile, learn what the world has to offer beyond the borders of this house, of this town, of this state.

It is a Sunday afternoon and I'm sitting in my backyard on a beach towel in a sweatshirt and sweatpants. This is the first weekend that feels like fall. I desperately want to take off my layers and feel the sun on my skin, but the breeze is too cold. So I sit and watch the wind bend the tree branches, watch the sun tint the grass a bright lime, watch the bees buzz around the little white-flowered weeds and contemplate whether or not I am happy.

You. You are someone who makes me crazy, who makes me feel important, who makes me feel special. But all I care about is whether I feel those things about myself. I close my eyes and imagine myself places—concerts, working my dream job, living in a beautifully-decorated apartment in the heart of a pulsing city—in each of those scenarios, I am alone.

It's not you, it's me. It's the fact that I want more than these days, these weekends. It's the fact that my dreams are too big. But it is not me. It's the way I deserve dinner dates and movie nights at the theatre where you'll dress up in jeans. It's the stargazing night you promised, the bike ride we still haven't taken, the board games and the coloring and the things I've wished for and been too disappointed to ask for again. It's afternoons in the September sun, holding the last slivers of summer close to our chests while talking about our futures, eating homemade pizza, and kissing tomato sauce of each other's fingers.

Maybe it's not me at all. On this little towel, with the sun warming my face and bare toes, I feel whole. I want you to love me like that sun, soothing but constant. Something I notice, even with a sweatshirt and sweatpants. Something I need. Something there when I need it. Something I crave. Something that fills me. And something that when I close my eyes, is still there. Still returns morning after morning and wherever I wander, however I change, still warms my face and my toes the same.

15

To The Next Girl He Loves

We have more in common than you think.

You must have brown hair, because he's partial to brunettes. And you must be hardworking and sassy, or a combination of both, because those are the type of girls he goes for.

You must love his laugh, and that little half-smirk he makes when you say something funny. You must love his hair, and how he always runs his fingers through it, just like that. You must love his eyes, and how they look both at you and through you somehow. You must like the way his hand feels on your skin, cold and warm and dangerous and comforting because somehow he makes all those things possible in a single brush of your waist.

I hope you always tell the jokes that make him laugh and watch the shows he likes. I hope you don't cook anything with spaghetti sauce because he hates it, and if you make chili, that you take out all the tomato chunks. I hope that you stay up late telling each other about your pasts and count the stars from the ledge outside his roof. I hope he tells you he loves you one day, but that it's romantic. That it makes you wonder if it's real. I think it will be.

I hope you argue, but I don't say this out of spite. I hope you challenge each other with your opinions and make each other think. I hope things don't come too easy, but that you fight and choose each other every day. That you force each other to answer the big questions—love, the future, what it all means. And I hope you don't take of those half-smirks, nights curled on the couch, dinners with the tomato-free sauce for granted. Because those will always be the best nights. The simplest nights.

This is my love letter to the both of you. I hope you find happiness. I hope you tease and laugh and travel together and that when you kiss there's tiny fireworks that erupt in the back of your brains like electric shocks.

I can't hate you. I won't. Because no matter how much I can't stand the thought of your lips on his, I'd rather see him happy. And because we're more alike than I thought, you and I. And I really can't hate you for that.

16

This Is The Incredible Power Of Love After Loss

In a single second you can cross a street, you can whisper *I love you*, you can take off in an airplane, you can feel your stomach drop, you can smile, or you can watch someone you love take his last breath. In a second, a tragic, slow-moving, catastrophic second, a friend of mine experienced the latter. She sat powerless as her best friend, her other half, her fiancé, her whole life breathed air for the last time then disappeared underwater.

Her fiancé was in a boat when it overturned. Two hours later, he was pulled from 12ft deep water. This accident occurred just a month prior to his graduation from college.

It breaks my heart, not knowing what to say, not having the words to heal or even begin to mend my friend's heart in the wake of such an enormous loss. But as I watched her, this beautiful girl with a smile that managed to find its way across her face, a laugh that still surfaced somehow, and a heart that was so pure and gold, I realized that this story, her story, is not a tragic story. **It will never be a tragic story.**

This story is not about loss, but about the incredible power of love. How love can lift us up when we're shattered into millions of tiny pieces, when we're struggling and gasping for a chance to survive in the aftermath of losing someone we've built a life, a future with. How love can heal and mend and smooth over the cracked pieces. How love changes us and our hearts and the world because it doesn't stop when a life does.

This beautiful friend of mine could have given up at any moment. And everyone expected her to. It wasn't because they doubted the person she was, but they couldn't see how she could pick up the bits of brokenness and make them whole again. How could she possibly continue when this was the only life she had known? How could she push on when the entire direction of who she was had suddenly changed? How could she look forward when there was nothing to focus on or trust?

But she did. Somehow she gathered the fragments of herself and put them back together. She pushed and pressed and forged on, all the while loving. Never forgetting. See, this isn't a story of death or a story of loss. It is a story of new beginnings. How this strong woman could pick herself up, how her love could create something beautiful despite her loss.

This young woman never gave up. When she had mended herself enough to talk, she talked. She cried. She opened herself to others and let them in. She shared her story, and shared it again and again and again until her story brought awareness. But she didn't stop there. She continued. She talked to friends and adults, she made phone calls to the college, to companies, to foundations, to people in high places that could make a difference. And she did.

She raised money for diving gear for the town, enough for two diving suits so that the emergency/rescue teams could be prepared if there ever was another emergency. She raised enough money for equipment, to help people respond to this type of crisis. She could have been bitter. She could have been angry that the world was unprepared for her situation, her tragedy. But she wasn't. She focused only on the good that could come out of it, the difference that she could make for the future.

See, that's why this isn't a sad story. It is not about loss, but about love. How love can turn loss into a gift, how something terrible and tragic can be molded into something beautiful, and how we somehow find ways to continue on, to break through the surface and start again, because we know that's what the people we lose would want us to do. And we love them, so we do just that.

17

You Broke My Heart, But I Am Forever Thankful

I wasn't supposed to fall in love with you. You were dangerous eyes and a quick temper. You were argumentative and stubborn and so wonderfully compassionate. I got lost in those eyes and felt safe in those arms.

We began as nothing. I told myself we were just having fun. That smiles were because we enjoyed each other's company. That kisses were playful. That we were happy, not falling.

I never meant to kiss so deeply. I never imagined that your arms around me would feel like home. And I don't know if you did either. Maybe it was a line we accidentally crossed, dancing in a bar just a little after midnight, the voices around us all melting away. Dancing, spinning, spinning. Or maybe it was when we explored each other's minds on a couch in your living room, confessing secrets we'd been too afraid to share. Opening slowly, learning to trust again.

I wasn't supposed to fall in love with you, but I did. Layer by layer. And I think you did, too. It happened exactly like the world says, slowly, then all at once. Suddenly we were sharing pillows and paychecks and dreams. Suddenly those three words, the 'I love yous' whispered at night, in the morning, as I dropped you off, when you picked me up, carried incredible weight.

But then we unfolded, as beautiful things often do. We were both at fault, maybe more than we wanted to admit. We fought hard. Me with words. You with those dangerous eyes, that quick temper. We cracked, shattered into tiny pieces that were too difficult to put back together, but a part of me still believed.

But then came the heartbreak. It was unexpected, yet a part of me knew it was inevitable. I had fallen. I was breakable. I wasn't supposed to be in love with you. I wasn't supposed to be hurt. But I was, just the same. And you had transformed into someone I no longer knew, someone I didn't think you were anymore, someone I never thought you could be. It broke me. It unraveled me into little threads of myself. Little fragments of my heart that I knew would take so long to mold back together.

But I forgave you.

In time. After tears. As I woke to the sun on a new day and saw the freedom, the lifted weight on my heart, in forgiving you. You were the boy with dangerous eyes, with arms that sheltered me. You were the boy whose home I discovered, whose heart I opened. The boy who had held my own heart in his hands. Together we had re-learned how to love, how to let someone in when you are still fragile, still scared. We had fallen in love. And because of this, I am forever thankful.

I am thankful for poolside drinks, for dog walks, for drives with the windows down. I am thankful for the swing you built me in the backyard, for the smell of your deodorant, for the picture frame in your room with the photos of us, laughing, smiling, dancing, spinning, spinning.

You broke my heart, but I am forever thankful. For the moments, the memories, the kisses, and the accidental falling that happens when you close your eyes, when you let it. For what I learned in losing you: what I deserve, the immensity of my strength, my capacity to love, to let go. For you. I hope you know that you are forgiven. But I still hope when you kiss her, you taste me. And I hope that one day you forgive yourself.

18

This Is What Is Left When You Lose Someone You Love

Look into my eyes.
Brush the hair back from my face. Kiss
me. Kiss my lips. Again.
Tell me
not that you love me,
but how the summer breeze blows
through those white blinds.
Tell me of the sausage and onion pizza
you ate for dinner last night,
the stupid joke your boss told during break,
your impossible fear of spiders.
I don't know, exactly,
what it is I want to hear.
But I know I like
the sound of your voice,
the way you grab my chin, and pull
my face to yours, stare
into my eyes.
As if this moment, this
single,

insignificant
moment
should be celebrated, remembered.
So that months later,
when you're gone
and I'm driving the highway alone,
suitcase in the passenger seat,
I remember those blinds, those eyes.
And I remember what I think I've always known.
It is the small moments
we carry with us.

19

I Made A Million And One Mistakes Loving Him, And I Will Make Them All Again

I loved. I lost. I fought hard. I argued. I compromised bits of myself for the sake of love.

I changed my mind. I went back on my word. I became a different version of myself, lost myself, and found myself again.

I was too stubborn. Too forgiving. Too harsh. Too gentle. I gave in. I gave up. I went back when I shouldn't have. And let go too soon.

I made a million and one mistakes loving him. But I don't regret a single one.

He came into my life with quickness and charm, both quiet and loud. I should have been stronger in the beginning. I should have been firm, stood my ground. But I caved. I tripped, slipped, and fell headfirst into love.

I should have put on the brakes. Should have stopped myself. Should have closed my eyes and let it happen slow, filling me, settling into my roots like a plant baking in the sun. But I didn't. I won't ever. The mistake I made in falling hard, I'd do it over, every time. For him. For the next love, and for the other loves that will come after.

I will make the mistake of kissing too deeply, of confessing too much, of letting someone touch the parts of my soul I try so hard to keep hidden. And I won't regret it.

I will make the mistake of trusting, make the mistake of intertwining my life and dreams with another. I will do this willingly, because this is love. Because this is beautiful.

In loving him, I made the mistake of losing myself. Not in a terrible way, but in the way that comes with love, when parts of yourself twist around that person. When who you are shapes, and is shaped, by your relationship. You are still whole, still complete, yet even more of yourself with that person. That is a mistake, with him, I willingly made. And I will make it again, wrapping my heart around my next love. Learning to give and take, once more.

I made the mistake of running when I couldn't face my anger. The mistake of shutting off when I should have spoken, of shouting when I should have been silent. These are mistakes of passion, mistakes of the moment, mistakes that define who I am, and mistakes that I cannot apologize for. I am human. I am me. I will do the same thing, every time. When you love someone you cannot help your reaction. So I will make these mistakes again. Make them when I'm angry. Make them when

I'm scared. Make them when I fall in love in the future, whenever that may be.

I have never been afraid to love. To be vulnerable. To give. To gain. To lose.

I have never been afraid of making mistakes. Even when I make them, time and time again. Even when they hurt just the same. This is a cycle that to me, will always be worth it. This is love, and I will keep on loving.

20

10 Reasons Why The Best Relationship Of Your Life Will Be With A Girl Who Loves 'Too Much'

1. She will bring incredible positivity to your life.

She loves you, she loves the world, and this love fills her every cell and bone and muscle and curve. Her love shines through her normal, everyday existence and it will be so bright and positive that every single day you will be encouraged.

2. She will get you over any past relationship, hurt, or trust issue.

She loves you too much for you to be thinking of any other female. She's the one whose presence unintentionally demands your attention. She distracts you with her mind, with her happiness, with her smile. She will love you so deeply that any past scars and any past pain will fade. You will forget the brokenness, the bad relationships of your past and with her, learn to love again.

3. She will show you what love really feels like.

Not the half-love you've known. Not the love that fades when times get tough, or when someone new comes along. Instead, she will love you consistently, patiently, willingly, and fearlessly through the ups and downs. She won't pull away. She won't run. She will love you in a way that fills the empty spaces of your life and makes you a more whole, more complete version of yourself.

4. She will never let you feel empty.

She will continually fill you with her love—on bad days, on tough mornings, after incredible loss, during the most difficult times. With her, you will never feel unsatisfied, never feel lonely. She will be all in, and more.

5. She will teach you forgiveness.

She loves the world and keeps loving the world, even when she sees its brokenness. She will forgive the evils done to her, and in her example, she will teach you. She will show you how to release your grip on the tiny, painful pieces you cannot control. She will show you how to pull the hurt from your bones and toss it into the wind. With her, you will learn to heal, you will learn to let go, and you will learn how freeing this process is.

6. She will be fiercely loyal to you.

A girl that loves 'too much' will never run out of love for you. She will value you, so much so that she would never do anything to hurt you. She may love the world, but that is not the love she shares with you—that love is sacred.

7. She'll open your heart to emotions.

She is emotional. She has feelings, and she's not scared of being open and honest about them. She is the type of girl who will peel back your layers and expose the parts of you that you try to keep hidden. She will show you the raw, unedited version of herself and in turn, you will do the same, learning to love in the realist, most beautiful way.

8. She's going to fight with you and more importantly, for you.

Because she loves you, she will fight with you. She will argue, she will challenge you, she will push you, and she will drive you crazy. But this is because she cares about you. She cares enough to go through hell together, just to come out on the other side even closer, even stronger. And she will fight for you. She will be your partner, your ride-or-die, your other half, fighting against the world for your love.

9. She will always choose to work through problems rather than walk away.

Her love is too much, but that doesn't mean your relationship will be perfect. You will have problems, but she will always choose to talk, to hash things out, to compromise, to work through the gritty stuff. She won't pack her bags and walk the second things get hard; she loves you, so she's all in.

10. She'll love your darkest places.

The unforgivable places. The places and memories and regrets and thoughts you keep hidden in the shadowy corners of your mind—she will love those. Her love will be the light that breaks through that darkness, cleans the cobwebs from what you've shoved away and tried to forget. She will love you and all that you come with—your past, your insecurities, your fears, and your evils.

21

Love Is Easy, It's Loving That's Hard

I spent four hours talking with my two best girlfriends about love. All three of us are at similar stages in our lives: finished with college, single, living somewhat on our own, semi-heartbroken, semi-in love, feeling the urge to wander.

The conversation happened on a Saturday morning at an outdoor cafe in Wrigleyville, each of us with different degrees of a hangover, all picking at the scraps of food left on our plates.

I'm not sure how the talking began, but my girlfriend started explaining this 'soul connection' her and her ex have. I don't know what the hell a soul connection is, but it sounded beautiful, like something you wouldn't want to lose.

"It's like your hearts just know each other," she explained.

And sitting there, I couldn't understand how she could know and feel all this, yet not actively pursue this person. In fact, she was the one who had broken it off.

She said that the communication between her and the ex was the issue. They would go days without talking and he would justify it with, 'Well you know I love you. We don't need to talk every day.'

Now that's the sort of thing that just pisses me off. I've heard that phrase before (one too many times). And if you ask me, I'll fully admit to being nosy. I want to know not only the big things in my significant other's life, but also the little things--*what'd you eat for dinner? who did you go out to the movies with? anything different happen at work?* And I don't think there's anything wrong with that. So listening to her explain her ex's justification, I could understand why she was frustrated. There's that part of you that just wants to know, just feels that if someone loves you they'll want to talk, even if it is just about the little things.

She explained how even though she felt such a love for her ex, the type of love she'd never felt before, she knew she couldn't be with him. For her, the communication problem was just too much to push off to the side. She knew the two of them weren't meant to be because she couldn't compromise on something she felt so strongly about. And on his end, he wouldn't meet her halfway.

The conversation got me thinking. Love is a powerful thing. And it's also difficult as hell. We give our hearts to another person, but we expect the same thing in return. The problem is, people love differently. And the hard part is trying to understand how people love, and to love them back, but also realizing when people don't love you how you need to be loved, *that matters.*

I've grown up believing that love isn't selfish. In fact, my best friend said it about her own situation—"*love is selfless.*" But I'm not sure I agree.

A selfless love means putting someone else's needs before your own. It means moving across the country to be with your significant other, even if you're settled in a place you consider home. It means putting your communication needs aside and giving your partner the benefit of the doubt. And I don't know if I agree with that.

Listening to my friend explain how hard her breakup was, but how she needed to do it because she couldn't forgo what she felt in her heart, left me with mixed feelings. I admired her strength, that she was able to walk away from what she wanted because she knew there was something better out there for her. But I was also pained, because I knew it killed her to wake up every day without the person she loved, knowing he was only a minute's walk away, but she couldn't talk to him.

I'm not sure if love is selfless. The first step to loving someone is to love yourself. And loving yourself is *selfish*. Loving yourself means knowing what you deserve and not being afraid to claim that. Loving yourself means staying planted where you are and pursuing the job you want. Loving yourself means not accepting bare-bones communication. It means not settling. But if everyone is loving themselves, no one could ever love someone else fully because there'd never be a compromise.

How can you truly love another person if you're always wanting to love yourself, to honor your own needs and desires?

But reverse that, if you're always trying to honor your significant other's needs and desires, you'll never pursue yours. Selfless yes, but unhappy.

At this point in the conversation, I leaned back in my chair and surveyed the cafe and everything else around us. Across the street was a playground. There were children screaming, a background noise that I hadn't noticed before. To our left was a mother, grandmother, and infant. The baby was pale white with blue veins on his head and beautiful blue eyes. Being a mother is selfless love, constantly putting someone else's needs before your own. But a child is dependent. That makes it different somehow.

"*Love is hard,*" I said. My friend was putting the leftover half of her sandwich into a to-go box.

"*No,*" she said, and stopped messing with her food to look up at me, "*love is easy.*"

I had looked away then, looked back across the street at the children. They were yelling and scrambling across the monkey bars. They weren't heartbroken or worried if they would ever fall in love again. They were just content on existing. On playing with chalk and waiting for the next meal. They were simple. And they were inherently and innocently selfish.

"*The act of love is easy,*" I said, thinking of how simple it was to see a person, to feel strongly for them, to want to be by their side, to want to give them everything. "*It's loving that's hard.*"

We sat at that cafe for a few more minutes. I thought about

that idea, the idea that love comes naturally, but loving, learning to love, learning to find the balance between give and take, a combination of selfish and selfless--that was hard.

Maybe love is about being selfish when it comes to finding the right person, because you need to find someone who's right for you. Maybe not. Maybe you'll know you're with the right person because you won't have to be selfish. You'll both be so sel*fless* that somehow you'll end up in the middle, both making sacrifices, willing and happy sacrifices, that you'll both end up with what you want. You'll want to move across the country for them, but they won't let you. Somehow you'll find a middle ground, and no one will be settling.

Perhaps love is difficult with the wrong person. It's easy to love them, to want to be with them, to crave that soul connection. But loving them is hard because they're not the one.

Who knows? We really don't know.

All I know from sitting at that cafe on a Saturday morning, is that love has to have a happy medium. You have to be selfish about what you want, but more importantly about what you deserve. But you need to love, and never stop loving. You just have to stumble ahead, opening your heart again and again, hoping it'll all work out, never giving up, believing in this ridiculously difficult, but beautiful piece of what it means to be human.

22

I'm A Spoiled Brat Because I Want You To Love Me As Much As I Love You

I'm a spoiled brat because I crave your attention. Your arms linked around my waist when we stand in front of the stove, alternating between stirring the pasta sauce and kissing. Your hand in mine when we walk into the bar on a Friday night, and you introduce me to your friends. Your fingers running through my hair when we curl up on the couch on a lazy Sunday afternoon.

Because I want to hear about your day—the sh*tty sandwich you got at the deli next door, the coworker who took another thirty minute bathroom break before lunch, the sedan with the duct-taped passenger door that cut you off on your way home.

Because I want your eye contact when we speak. No video games. No cell phones. No computer screens. Just me and you, your brown eyes locked on my face.

I'm a spoiled brat because I want you to do things with me.

Because I don't always want to be the one to make the plans, to pay for the dinner dates, to come up with things for the two of us to do. I want you to think ahead sometimes, to buy groceries, to make reservations, to grab my hand and pull me back to the car the second I walk in the front door, my night already mapped out.

I'm a spoiled brat because I want text messages. Some in the morning. Some during your lunch. Even a few at night, when we're both driving home. Little things, 'How's your day, Babe?' 'Hey, just thinking of you.' And even some messages back when I text you.

Because I want to hear what's on your mind, the random things you're thinking about, how your favorite pro basketball team's doing, what you want to eat for dinner.

Because I want to hear your perspectives, and discover the way you think.

Because I want to be challenged to think differently, to argue with you about our passions and learn even more about each other.

I'm a spoiled brat because I want you—physically and mentally, the good and the bad, the lazy days and the adventures.

I'm a spoiled brat because I want you to love me as much as I love you.

23

It's Okay To Love Fiercely (And Expect Fierce Love In Return)

It's okay to love fiercely and expect that in return.

To love with passion. The kind that pulls back the window blinds and lets in the sun. The radio dial turned to max, hands up, and the windows down.

When you fall, it's okay to fall deeply. To see yourself, your life intertwined in the pages, the roads, the curves of your significant other.

It's okay to believe words. The words that you've heard before, that twisted themselves in your mind, that kept you up at night, spinning, spinning. It's okay to trust those words, again and again.

And it's okay to say those words. And mean them. The 'I love yous' on the tip of your tongue, the lines you've kept hidden. It's okay to say them. To speak them. To shout them. To unravel what's in your head, fearlessly. To let someone in, fully in.

You are not crazy. You are not foolish if you love with abandon. If you throw yourself headfirst into his eyes, run your fingertips across his collarbone before he draws you into a kiss, memorize the freckles on his back.

You are not wrong for the craziness you feel. The excitement at a simple touch, a smile, a small gesture. It's okay to hold onto a hug for just a moment too long, to stay in bed an extra minute, just to feel his touch on your skin.

It's okay to love fiercely. To demand things. To demand communication. To demand that you spend time together. To demand the best for himself, yourself, your relationship.

It's okay to love someone intensely, even too intensely. To look at them and see your world, to see your lives years down the road, to imagine a future, paved and imperfect and beautiful.

Your love is big. It fills the cracks, the faults, the flaws. It seals over the fights, fixes every broken piece. Your love covers the surface then seeps into the pores. You have a love that's embedded in your soul. You love fiercely, with everything you have.

And you expect this in return.

You crave his touch, his voice, his love in all its forms. Your love is too big to settle for anything that is not full love, real love. And so you expect his love to match yours, for your lives to be interconnected, one.

This is okay. It's okay to love fiercely, to expect fierce love. You need this type of love. You are not wrong. You deserve this love, a love that matches yours, that ignites fires, that lights fireworks, that grows and builds and sings like the radio with the dial turned loud.

No, don't apologize. You are not too much. You will never be too much.

Thought Catalog, it's a website.
www.thoughtcatalog.com

Social
facebook.com/thoughtcatalog
twitter.com/thoughtcatalog
tumblr.com/thoughtcatalog

Corporate
www.thought.is

Made in the USA
Middletown, DE
17 January 2020